Beautiful Baby SHOES

General Information

Many of the products used in this pattern book can be purchased from local craft, fabric and variety stores.

Contents

Kimono Slippers

SKILL LEVEL

INTERMEDIATE

FINISHED SIZES

Instructions given fit size newborn–3 months (*small*); changes for sizes 3–6 months (*medium*), 6–12 months (*large*) and 12–18 months (*X-large*) are in [ ].

FINISHED MEASUREMENTS

Sole: 3 inches (*small*) [3½ inches (*medium*), 4 inches (*large*), 4½ inches (*X-large*)]

MATERIALS

- Super fine (fingering) weight yarn: 1¾ oz/309 yds/50g each bright pink, pale pink and bright green for all sizes
- Size D/3/3.25mm crochet hook or size needed to obtain gauge
- Sewing needle
- Matching sewing thread

1
SUPER FINE

GAUGE

6 sc = 1 inch; 6 sc rows = 1 inch

PATTERN NOTES

You may want to apply a rubber backing on bottom of Sole for toddler sizes if used on floors other than carpet.

The 11 skipped single crochet at front of toe are worked off 1 at a time at beginning and end of each row. Working in front loops and back loops creates the overlapping kimono-style effect after all 11 single crochet are worked and 11 rows of Sides are completed.

Join with slip stitch as indicated unless otherwise stated.

SPECIAL STITCH

Surface stitch (surface st): Holding yarn at back of work, insert hook between sts, yo, pull lp through st and lp on hook.

INSTRUCTIONS
SLIPPER
MAKE 2.
SOLE

Row 1: With bright pink, ch 7 [8, 8, 8], sc in 2nd ch from hook and in each ch across, turn. (*6 [7, 7, 7] sc*)

Rows 2–5 [2–6, 2–7, 2–8]: Ch 1, sc in each st across, turn.

Row 6 [7, 8, 9] (inc): Ch 1, 2 sc in first st, sc in each st across with 2 sc in last st, turn. (*8 [9, 9, 9] sc*)

Rows 7–10 [8–12, 9–14, 10–16]: Ch 1, sc in each st across, turn.

Row 11 [13, 15, 17] (inc): Ch 1, 2 sc in first st, sc in each st across with 2 sc in last st, turn. (*10 [11, 11, 11] sc*)

Rows 12–15 [14–18, 16–21, 18–24]: Ch 1, sc in each st across, turn.

Rows 16 & 17 [19 & 20, 22 & 23, 25 & 26] (dec): Ch 1, sc in first st, sk next st, sc in each st across to last 2 sts, sk next st, sc in last st, turn. At end of last row, **do not fasten off.** (*6 [7, 7, 7] sc at end of last row*)

EDGING

Working in sts, ends of rows and in starting ch on opposite side of row 1, ch 1, evenly sp sc around, **join** (*see Pattern Notes*) in beg sc. Fasten off.

LEFT SLIPPER
SIDES

Row 1: Working in **back lps** (*see Stitch Guide*), **sk 11 sc at front of toe** (*see Pattern Notes*), join light pink with sc in next st, sc in each st across to first sk sts, sl st in **front lp** (*see Stitch Guide*) of next st at front of toe, leaving rem sts unworked, turn.

Row 2: Ch 1, sc in same st, sc in both lps of each st across to opposite side, sc in front lp of next sk sc at front of toe, sl st in front lp of next sk st at front of toe, turn.

Rows 3–6: Rep row 2.

Rows 7–11: Ch 1, sc in same st, sc in both lps of each st across to opposite side, sc in rem lp of next sc at front of toe, sl st in rem lp of next sc at front of toe, turn. At end of last row, fasten off.

RIGHT SLIPPER
SIDES

Row 1: Working in **back lps**, **sk 11 sc to right of join at front of toe** (*see Pattern Notes*), join light pink with sc in next st, sc in each st across to sk sts, sl st in back lp of next st at front of toe, leaving the rem sc unworked, turn.

Row 2: Ch 1, sc in same st, sc in both lps of each st across to opposite side, sc in back lp of next sk sc at front of toe, sl st in back lp of next sk sc at front of toe, turn.

Rows 3–6: Rep row 2.

Rows 7–11: Rep rows 7–11 of Left Slipper.

SIDE TRIM

With RS facing, **join** (*see Pattern Notes*) bright pink at 1 end of row 11, evenly sp sl st across to opposite side of row 11. Fasten off.

FINISHING

Fold rows at toe so that they meet at 9th or 10th st of row 11, using sewing needle and sewing thread, sew tog along overlap seam to secure.

FLOWER BUTTON

Rnd 1: With light pink, ch 2, 5 sc in 2nd ch from hook. Fasten off.

Rnd 2: Working in back lps, join bright pink in any sc, (ch 2, 2 dc, ch 2, sl st) in same st (*petal*), (sl st, ch 2, 2 dc, ch 2, sl st) in each st around, join in beg sl st. Fasten off.

Sew Flower Button in place at outer top side of Shoe, 7 or 8 sts further back from place where toe joins.

FLOWER STEM BUTTON LOOP

Join bright green near bottom inner side of Shoe, **surface st** (*see Special Stitch*) up side of Shoe to top, ch 11, sl st in 10th ch from hook, sl st in next ch, sl st in top of Shoe to secure. Fasten off. ∎

Casual Baby Sandals

SKILL LEVEL

INTERMEDIATE

FINISHED SIZES

Instructions given fit size newborn (*small*); changes for sizes 0–6 months (*medium*), sizes 6–12 months (*large*) and 12–18 months (*X-large*) are in [ ].

FINISHED MEASUREMENTS

Sole: 3 inches (*small*) [3¾ inches (*medium*), 4¼ inches (*large*), 4¾ inches (*X-large*)]

MATERIALS

- Medium (worsted) weight cotton yarn:
  1¾ oz/88 yds/50g each dark brown and blue for all sizes
- Size F/5/3.75mm crochet hook or size needed to obtain gauge
- Sewing needle
- Matching sewing thread
- Small buttons: 2
- Stitch markers

4 MEDIUM

GAUGE

5 sc = 1 inch; 5 sc rows = 1 inch

PATTERN NOTES

You may want to apply a rubber backing on bottom of Sole for toddler sizes if used on floors other than carpet.

Chain-2 at beginning row or round counts as first double crochet unless otherwise stated.

Join with slip stitch as indicated unless otherwise stated.

INSTRUCTIONS
SANDAL
MAKE 2.
SOLE

Row 1: With blue, ch 7, sc in 2nd ch from hook and in each ch across, turn.

Rows 2–4 [2–5, 2–6, 2–7]: Ch 1, sc in each st across, turn.

Row 5 [6, 7, 8] (inc): Ch 1, 2 sc in first st, sc in each st across with 2 sc in last st, turn. (*8 [8, 8, 8] sc*)

Rows 6–8 [7–10, 8–12, 9–14]: Ch 1, sc in each st across, turn.

Row 9 [11, 13, 15] (inc): Ch 1, 2 sc in first st, sc in each st across with 2 sc in last st, turn. *(10 [10, 10, 10] sc)*

Rows 10–12 [12–15, 14–18, 16–21]: Ch 1, sc in each st across, turn.

Rows 13 & 14 [16 & 17, 19 & 20, 22 & 23] (dec): Ch 1, sc in first st, sk next st, sc in each st across to last 2 sts, sk next st, sc in last st, turn. At end of last row, **do not fasten off**. *(6 [6, 6, 6] sc at end of last row)*

SOLE EDGING
Rnd 1: Working in sts, ends of rows and in starting ch on opposite side of row 1, ch 1, evenly sp sc around, **join** *(see Pattern Notes)* in beg sc.

Rnd 2: Ch 1, sc in each st around, join in beg sc. Fasten off.

INSOLE
With dark brown, work same as Sole.

SMALL & MEDIUM SIZES ONLY
RIGHT FOOT
SIDES & HEEL
Row 1: Sk 14 sc at Insole toe, working in **back lps** *(see Stitch Guide)*, join dark brown with sc in next st, sc in each st across sides and back of Insole, turn.

Rows 2–5: Ch 1, sc in each st across, turn. At end of last row, **do not fasten off**.

STRAP
Row 1: Ch 1, sc in each of first 5 sts, leaving rem sts unworked, turn.

Rows 2–10: Ch 1, sc in each st across, turn.

Row 11: Ch 1, sc in each of first 2 sts, ch 1, sk next st *(buttonhole)*, sc in each of next 2 sts, turn.

Row 12: Ch 1, sc in each st and in each ch across. Fasten off.

LEFT FOOT
SIDES & HEEL
Row 1: Sk 14 sc at Insole toe, working in **back lps** *(see Stitch Guide)*, join dark brown with sc in opposite end of row 5, sc in each st across sides and back of Insole, turn.

Rows 2–5: Ch 1, sc in each st across, turn. At end of last row, **do not fasten off**.

STRAP
Row 1: Ch 1, sc in each of first 5 sts, leaving rem sts unworked, turn.

Rows 2–10: Ch 1, sc in each st across, turn.

Row 11: Ch 1, sc in each of first 2 sts, ch 1, sk next st *(buttonhole)*, sc in each of next 2 sts, turn.

Row 12: Ch 1, sc in each st and in each ch across. Fasten off.

LARGE & X-LARGE SIZES ONLY
RIGHT FOOT
SIDES & HEEL
Row 1: Sk 16 sc at Insole toe, working in **back lps** *(see Stitch Guide)*, join dark brown with sc in opposite end of row 5, sc in each st across sides and back of Insole, turn.

Rows 2–6: Ch 1, sc in each st across, turn. At end of last row, **do not fasten off**.

STRAP
Row 1: Ch 1, sc in each of first 5 sts, leaving rem sts unworked, turn.

Rows 2–10: Ch 1, sc in each st across, turn.

Row 11: Ch 1, sc in each of first 2 sts, ch 1, sk next st *(buttonhole)*, sc in each of next 2 sts, turn.

Row 12: Ch 1, sc in each st and in each ch across. Fasten off.

LEFT FOOT
SIDES & HEEL
Row 1: Sk 16 sc at Insole toe, working in **back lps** *(see Stitch Guide)*, join dark brown with sc in next st, sc in each st across sides and back of Insole, turn.

Rows 2–6: Ch 1, sc in each st across, turn. At end of last row, **do not fasten off**.

STRAP

Row 1: Ch 1, sc in each of first 5 sts, leaving rem sts unworked, turn.

Rows 2–10: Ch 1, sc in each st across, turn.

Row 11: Ch 1, sc in each of first 2 sts, ch 1, sk next st *(buttonhole)*, sc in each of next 2 sts, turn.

Row 12: Ch 1, sc in each st and in each ch across. Fasten off.

FINISHING

With blue, sl st evenly around Sides and Strap as shown in photo.

Using sewing needle and sewing thread, sew button to Sides.

Holding Sole and Insole pieces tog, working through both thicknesses in **front lps** *(see Stitch Guide)* on Sole Edging and in back lps of Insole Edging, sl st pieces tog. Fasten off. ■

Knit-Look Sweater Boots

SKILL LEVEL

INTERMEDIATE

FINISHED SIZES

Instructions given fit size 0–6 months *(small)*; changes for size 6–12 months *(medium)* are in [ ].

FINISHED MEASUREMENTS

Sole: 3 inches *(small)* [3½ inches *(medium)*]

MATERIALS

- Super fine (fingering) weight yarn: 1¾ oz/309 yds/50g light pink for all sizes
- Fine (sport) weight yarn: 1¾ oz/176 yds/50g brown for all sizes
- Size D/3/3.25mm crochet hook or size needed to obtain gauge
- Tapestry needle

1 SUPER FINE

2 FINE

GAUGE

Fine weight yarn: 6 sc = 1 inch; 6 sc rows = 1 inch

PATTERN NOTES

You may want to apply a rubber backing on bottom of Sole for toddler sizes if used on floors other than carpet.

Cuff may be made to any length, just begin with an even number of chains.

Join with slip stitch as indicated unless otherwise stated.

INSTRUCTIONS
BOOT
MAKE 2.
SOLE

Row 1: With brown, ch 7, sc in 2nd ch from hook and in each ch across, turn. *(6 sc)*

Rows 2–5 [2–6]: Ch 1, sc in each st across, turn.

Row 6 [7] (inc): Ch 1, 2 sc in first st, sc in each st across with 2 sc in last st, turn. *(8 [8] sc)*

Rows 7–10 [8–12]: Ch 1, sc in each st across, turn.

Row 11 [13] (inc): Ch 1, 2 sc in first st, sc in each st across with 2 sc in last st, turn. *(10 [10] sc)*

Rows 12–15 [14–18]: Ch 1, sc in each st across, turn.

Rows 16 & 17 [19 & 20] (dec): Ch 1, sc in first st, sk next st, sc in each st across to last 2 sts, sk next st, sc in last st, turn. At end of last row, **do not fasten off.** *(6 [6] sc at end of last row)*

EDGING

Working in sts, ends of rows and in starting ch on opposite side of row 1, ch 1, evenly sp sc around, **join** *(see Pattern Notes)* in beg sc. Fasten off.

CUFF

Row 1: With pink, **ch 14** *(see Pattern Notes)*, sc in 2nd ch from hook, [ch 1, sk next ch, sc in next ch] across, turn.

Row 2 (RS): This is a ribbed row, ch 1, sc in first st, ch 1, [**bpsc** *(see Stitch Guide)* around next st, ch 1] across, ending with sc in last st, turn.

Row 3 (WS): This is a ribbed row, ch 1, sc in first st, ch 1, [**fpsc** *(see Stitch Guide)* around next st, ch 1] across, ending with sc in last st, turn.

Rows 4 & 5: Rep rows 2 and 3.

Row 6: Ch 1, sc in first st, [ch 1, sc in next st] across, turn.

Row 7: This is a ribbed row, ch 1, sc in first st, ch 1, [fpsc around next st, ch 1] across, ending with sc in last st, turn.

Row 8: This is a ribbed row, ch 1, sc in first st, ch 1, [bpsc around next st, ch 1] across, ending with sc in last st, turn.

Rows 9 & 10: Rep rows 7 and 8.

Row 11: Ch 1, sc in first st, [ch 1, sc in next st] across, turn.

Next rows: Rep rows 2–11 consecutively until you have 6 ribbed sections, ending with row 10. **Do not turn** at end of last row.

CUFF EDGING

Row 1: Working in ends of rows of Cuff, evenly sp 35 sc across, turn.

Row 2 (eyelet): Ch 3 *(counts as first dc and ch-1)*, sk next st, dc in next st, [ch 1, sk next st, dc in next st] across, turn.

Row 3: Ch 1, sc in each st and in each ch sp across. Fasten off.

TOE

Row 1: Sk first 12 sts on last row of Cuff Edging, join with sc in next st, sc in each of next 10 sts, leaving rem sts unworked, turn. *(11 sc)*

Rows 2–11 [2–15]: Ch 1, sc in each st across, turn.

Rows 12 & 13 [16 & 17] (dec): Ch 1, sc in first st, sk next st, sc in each st across to last 2 sts, sk next st, sc in last st, turn. At end of last row, fasten off. *(7 [7] sc at end of last row)*

SIDES

Row 1: Join pink with sc in first unworked sc of row 3 on Cuff Edging, sc in each of next 11 sts, working in ends of rows on Toe, sc in end of each row across, sc in each of next 7 sts across last row of Toe, working in rem ends of rows, sc in end of each row across Toe, sc in each of last 12 sts of row 3 on Cuff Edging, turn.

Rows 2–5: Ch 1, sc in each st across, turn.

Row 6: With WS tog, sl st ends of rows tog for seam at heel, sl st in 2 chs at end of eyelet row to leave eyelet sp open at back of heel. Fasten off.

FINISHING
Holding Sides and Sole pieces tog with Sides facing, working through both thicknesses, sl st pieces tog. Fasten off.

TIE
With brown, leaving small length at end, ch 85 or desired length. Leaving small length, fasten off.

Tie knot in each end.

Beg at center front of Boot, weave Tie through ch sps on eyelet row.

Tie ends in bow. ∎

Side-Button
Boots

SKILL LEVEL

INTERMEDIATE

FINISHED SIZES
Instructions given fit size newborn *(small)*; changes for sizes 0–6 months *(medium)*, 6–12 months *(large)* and 12–18 months *(X-large)* are in [ ].

FINISHED MEASUREMENTS
Sole: 3 inches *(small)* [3½ inches *(medium)*, 4 inches *(large)*, 4½ inches *(X-large)*]

MATERIALS
- Medium (worsted) weight cotton yarn: 1¾ oz/88 yds/50g each tan and chocolate for all sizes
- Size F/5/3.75mm crochet hook or size needed to obtain gauge
- Sewing needle
- Matching sewing thread
- Small buttons: 2
- Stitch markers

GAUGE
5 sc = 1 inch; 5 sc rows = 1 inch

PATTERN NOTES
You may want to apply a rubber backing on bottom of Sole for toddler sizes if used on floors other than carpet.

Chain-2 at beginning row or round counts as first double crochet unless otherwise stated.

Join with slip stitch as indicated unless otherwise stated.

INSTRUCTIONS
BOOT
MAKE 2.
SOLE
Row 1: With tan, ch 7, sc in 2nd ch from hook and in each ch across, turn. *(6 sc)*

Rows 2–4 [2-5, 2-6, 2-7]: Ch 1, sc in each st across, turn.

Row 5 [6, 7, 8] (inc): Ch 1, 2 sc in first st, sc in each st across with 2 sc in last st, turn. *(8 [8, 8, 8] sc)*

Rows 6–8 [7-10, 8-12, 9-14]: Ch 1, sc in each st across, turn.

Row 9 [11, 13, 15] (inc): Ch 1, 2 sc in first st, sc in each st across with 2 sc in last st, turn. *(10 [10, 10, 10] sc)*

Rows 10–12 [12-15, 14-18, 16-21]: Ch 1, sc in each st across, turn.

Rows 13 & 14 [16 & 17, 19 & 20, 22 & 23] (dec): Ch 1, sc in first st, sk next st, sc in each st across to last 2 sts, sk next st, sc in last st, turn. At end of last row, **do not fasten off.** *(6 [6, 6, 6] sc at end of last row)*

SOLE EDGING
Rnd 1: Working in sts, ends of rows and in starting ch on opposite side of row 1, ch 1, evenly sp sc around, **join** *(see Pattern Notes)* in beg sc.

Rnds 2 & 3: Ch 1, sc in each st around, join in beg sc. At end of last rnd, fasten off.

SOLE TRIM
Working in sps between sts on rnd 2 of Sole Edging, join chocolate in first sp, sl st in each sp around, join in beg sl st. Fasten off.

RIGHT FOOT
SIDES
Row 1: Mark center 24 [28, 32, 36] sc at front of toe, join tan in next sc after last marked st on right-hand side of Sole, **ch 2** *(see Pattern Notes)*, dc in **back lp** *(see Stitch Guide)* of each of next 2 sts, dc in both lps of each st around to first marked sc, working across marked sts, hdc in next st, sc in each of next 7 [9, 11, 13] sts, sk next st, sc in each of next 6 sts, sk next st, sc in each of next 7 [9, 11, 13] sts, hdc in next st, dc in rem **front lps** *(see Stitch Guide)* of each of next 3 sts to overlap beg of row, turn.

Row 2: Ch 2, dc in each of next 2 sts, hdc in next st, [sc in each of next 6 [8, 10, 12] sts, sk next st] twice, sc in each of next 6 [8, 10, 12] sts, hdc in next st, hdc in each st across to back of heel, [**dc dec** *(see Stitch Guide)* in next 2 sts] 4 times in center 8 sts of heel, dc in each st across, turn.

Row 3: Ch 2, dc in each st across to opposite side, hdc in next hdc, sl st in back lp of each of next 18 [22, 26, 30] sc, hdc in next hdc, dc in each of last 3 sts. Fasten off.

TOE TOP
Row 1: With tan, ch 5, sc in 2nd ch from hook and in each ch across, turn.

Rows 2–6 [2-8, 2-10, 2-12]: Ch 1, sc in each st across, turn.

Rnd 7: Ch 1, sc in each st across, working in ends of rows, sc in end of each row across first side, working in starting ch on opposite side of row 1, sc each ch across, working in ends of rows, sc in each row across 2nd side, join in beg sc. Fasten off.

JOINING

Holding Toe Top and Sides tog, with Toe Top facing, working at top of 1 long side of Toe Top and joining with sc to front lps of hdc on 1 side of Sides, sc pieces tog, working in rem lps of row 3 on Sides, end by working in hdc on opposite side of Sides. Fasten off.

CUFF

Row 1: Join chocolate with sc in first dc of row 3 on Sides, sc in each dc across to opposite side of Sides, sc in each sc across Toe Top, sc in each of 3 dc at end of row, turn.

Rows 2–4: Ch 1, sc in each st across, turn.

Row 5: Ch 1, sl st in each sc across, **do not turn.**

BUTTON STRAP

Row 1: Working in ends of rows, ch 1, sc in end of each row across Cuff, turn. (*4 sc*)

Row 2: Ch 1, sc in each of first 2 sts, ch 2 (*buttonhole*), sc in each of last 2 sts, turn.

Row 3: Ch 1, sc in first sc, sk next st, 2 sc in next ch sp, sk next st, sc in last st. Fasten off.

FINISHING

Using sewing needle and sewing thread, sew button in place at top inside of Cuff opposite buttonhole as shown in photo.

LEFT FOOT
SIDES

Row 1: Mark center 24 [28, 32, 36] sc at front of toe, join tan in front lp of sc 3 sts before first marker on left-hand side of Sole, ch 2, dc in front lp of each of next 2 sts, working across marked sts, hdc in next st, sc in each of next 7 [9, 11, 13] sts, sk next st, sc in each of next 6 sts, sk next st, sc in each of next 7 [9, 11, 13] sts, hdc in next st, dc in each rem sc across, dc in back lps of each of next 3 sts to overlap the beg of row, turn.

Row 2: Ch 2, dc in each dc across to back of heel, [dc dec in next 2 sts] 4 times across center 8 sts at heel, dc in each dc across, hdc in next hdc, [sc in each of next 6 [8, 10, 12] sts, sk next st] twice, sc in each of next 6 [8, 10, 12] sts, hdc in next hdc, dc in each of last 3 sts, turn.

Row 3: Ch 2, dc in each of next 2 dc, hdc in next hdc, sl st in back lp of each of next 18 [22, 26, 30] sc, hdc in next hdc, dc in each dc across. Fasten off.

TOE TOP & JOINING

Work same as Right Foot Toe Top and Joining.

CUFF

Row 1: Join chocolate with sc in first dc of row 3 on Sides, sc in each of next 2 dc, sc in each of sc across Toe Top, sc in each dc across to opposite side, turn.

Rows 2–3: Ch 1, sc in each st across, turn.

Row 4: Ch 1, sc in each st across, **do not turn.**

BUTTON STRAP

Row 1: Working in ends of rows, ch 1, sc in end of each row across Cuff, turn. (*4 sc*)

Row 2: Ch 1, sc in each of first 2 sts, ch 2 (*buttonhole*), sc in each of last 2 sts, turn.

Row 3: Ch 1, sc in first sc, sk next st, 2 sc in next ch sp, sk next st, sc in last st, turn.

Row 4: Ch 1, sl st in each st across end of Button Strap and in each st across row 3 of Cuff. Fasten off.

FINISHING

Using sewing needle and sewing thread, sew button in place at top inside of Cuff opposite buttonhole as shown in photo. ∎

Two-Button Slippers

SKILL LEVEL

INTERMEDIATE

FINISHED SIZES

Instructions given fit sizes newborn–3 months
(*small*), 3–6 months (*medium*), 6–12 months
(*large*) and 12–18 months (*X-large*) according
to worked length of Sole.

FINISHED MEASUREMENTS

Sole: 3 inches (*small*) [3½ inches (*medium*),
4 inches (*large*), 4½ inches (*X-large*)]

MATERIALS

- Super fine (fingering) weight yarn:
  1¾ oz/309 yds/50g red for all sizes
- Size D/3/3.25mm crochet hook
  or size needed to obtain gauge
- Sewing needle
- Matching sewing thread
- Small buttons: 4

GAUGE

5 sc = 1 inch; 5 sc rows = 1 inch

PATTERN NOTES

You may want to apply a rubber backing on bottom of Sole for toddler sizes if used on floors
other than carpet.

Chain-2 at beginning row or round counts as first
double crochet unless otherwise stated.

Join with slip stitch as indicated unless
otherwise stated.

SPECIAL STITCH

Pleat: Insert hook in next st, sk next st, insert
hook from back to front through next st,
complete as sl st.

INSTRUCTIONS
SLIPPER
MAKE 2.
TOE

Rnd 1: Ch 4, sl st in beg ch to form ring, **ch 2** (*see
Pattern Notes*), 11 dc in ring, **join** (*see Pattern
Notes*) in 2nd ch of beg ch-2. (*12 dc*)

Row 2: Now working in rows, ch 2, dc in same st, 2 dc in each of next 5 sts, leaving rem sts unworked, turn. *(12 dc)*

Row 3: Ch 3 *(counts as first dc and ch-1)*, dc in next st, [ch 1, dc in next st] across, turn.

Row 4: Ch 1, sc in each st and in each ch across, turn. *(23 sc)*

Row 5: Ch 1, sc in each st across, turn.

Row 6: Ch 2, dc in next st, [**dc dec** *(see Stitch Guide)* in next 2 sts] 10 times, dc in last st, turn. *(13 dc)*

Row 7: Ch 1, dc in next st *(ch-1 and last dc count as first dec)*, [dc dec in next 2 sts] 5 times, leaving rem sts unworked, turn. *(6 dc)*

Row 8: Ch 1, **sc dec** *(see Stitch Guide)* in next 6 sts, **do not turn or fasten off.**

UPPER STRAPS

Ch 1, sc in end of next row, *2 sc in end of each of next 2 rows, sc in end of each of next 2 rows, 2 sc in end of each of next 2 rows*, working in 6 unworked sts of rnd 1 on Toe, [sc in each of next 2 sts, ch 10, sl st in 6th ch from hook and in each of next 4 chs] twice, sc in each of next 2 sts, rep between * once, sc in end of last row, join in beg sc. Fasten off.

SOLE

Row 1: With top of Toe facing, sk sc above row 1 of Toe, join with sc in first sc above row 2 on left side of Toe, sc in each sc across to opposite side of Toe, ending with last sc above row 2 on right side of Toe, turn. *(18 sc)*

Row 2: Ch 1, sc in each st across, turn.

Next rows: Rep row 2 until piece measures size length *(see Finished Measurements)*. At end of last row, fasten off.

HEEL

Row 1: Sk first 6 sts on last row of Sole, join with sc in next st, sc in each of next 4 sts, sc dec in next 2 sts, sl st in next st, leaving rem sts unworked, turn.

Row 2: Sk sl st, sc in each of next 5 sts, sc dec in last sc of row 1 and next unworked st on last row of Sole, sl st in next st on Sole, leaving rem sts unworked, turn.

Next rows: Rep row 2 until all sts on last row of Sole are worked, working last sl st of last row in same st as last st. At end of last row, fasten off.

UPPER EDGING

Row 1: Join with sc in end of row 2 on Sole, sc in end of each row across, side, back of heel and along opposite side, ending at other end of row 2, turn.

Row 2: Sl st in each st across, working 3 **pleats** *(see Special Stitch)* across 9 sts at back of heel. Fasten off.

FINISHING

Using sewing needle and sewing thread, sew buttons in place at either side of Upper Edging and pull lp over each button according to photo. ■

Daisy Baby Sandals

SKILL LEVEL

INTERMEDIATE

FINISHED SIZES

Instructions given fit size newborn–6 months
(*small*); changes for sizes 6–12 months
(*medium*), 12–18 months (*large*), 18–24 months
(*X-large*), 24–30 months (*2X-large*) and 30–36
months (*3X-large*) are in [ ].

FINISHED MEASUREMENTS

Sole: 3½ inches (*small*) [4 inches (*medium*), 4½
inches (*large*), 5 inches (*X-large*), 5½ inches
(*2X-large*), 6 inches (*3X-large*)]

MATERIALS

- Medium (worsted) weight yarn:
  1¾ oz/88 yds/50g tan for Sole and
  Ankle Loop for all sizes
- Fine (sport) weight yarn:
  1¾ oz/176 yds/50g each white,
  pink and yellow for Insole,
  Straps and Flower of all sizes
- Super fine (fingering) weight yarn:
  1¾ oz/300 yds/50g white for
  joining Sole and Insole for all sizes
- Size F/5/3.75mm crochet hook
  or size needed to obtain gauge
- Sewing needle
- Matching sewing thread
- Stitch markers

GAUGE

Medium weight yarn: 5 sc = 1 inch; 5 sc rows =
1 inch

PATTERN NOTES

You may want to apply a rubber backing on
bottom of Sole for toddler sizes if used on
floors other than carpet.

Work in back loops throughout unless
otherwise stated.

Chain-2 at beginning row or round counts as first
double crochet unless otherwise stated.

Join with slip stitch as indicated unless
otherwise stated.

INSTRUCTIONS
SANDAL
MAKE 2.
RIBBED SOLE

Row 1: With tan, ch 7 [8, 9, 9, 9, 9], sc in 2nd ch from hook and in each ch across, turn. (6 [7, 8, 8, 8, 8, 8] sc)

Rows 2–5 [2–6, 2–7, 2–8, 2–9, 2–10]: Working in **back lps** (see Stitch Guide and Pattern Notes), ch 1, sc in each st across, turn.

Row 6 [7, 8, 9, 10, 11] (inc): Ch 1, 2 sc in first st, sc in each st across with 2 sc in last st, turn. (8 [9, 10, 10, 10, 10] sc)

Rows 7–10 [8–12, 9–14, 10–16, 11–18, 12–20]: Ch 1, sc in each st across, turn.

Row 11 [13, 15, 17, 19, 21] (inc): Ch 1, 2 sc in first st, sc in each st across with 2 sc in last st, turn. (10 [11, 12, 12, 12, 12] sc)

Rows 12–15 [14–18, 16–21, 18–24, 20–27, 22–30]: Ch 1, sc in each st across, turn.

Rows 16 & 17 [19 & 20, 22 & 23, 25 & 26, 28 & 29, 31 & 32] (dec): Ch 1, sc in first st, sk next st, sc in each st across to last 2 sts, sk next st, sc in last st, turn. At end of last row, **do not fasten off.** (6 [6, 7, 8, 8, 8, 8] sc at end of last row)

EDGING
Working in sts, ends of rows and in starting ch on opposite side of row 1, ch 1, evenly sp sc around, **join** (see Pattern Notes) in beg sc. Fasten off.

INSOLE
Using pink, work same as Sole, working in both lps instead of back lps.

JOINING
Using super fine yarn, holding 1 Ribbed Sole piece and 1 Insole piece tog, with Ribbed Sole on bottom and Insole facing, working through both thicknesses and in back lps of Insole and **front lps** (see Stitch Guide) of Ribbed Sole, sl st around, join in beg sl st. Fasten off.

ANKLE LOOP
Row 1: Mark center 5 or 6 sts on heel, join tan with sc in first marked st, sc in each st across to next marker, turn.

Rows 2–12: Ch 1, sc in each st across, turn.

Last row: Fold row 12 in half toward inside of Sole, sl st in base of each st across row 1. Fasten off. ■

TOE STRAP
MAKE 2.
Using tan, make ch the same length as the length of the Sole, sl st in 2nd ch from hook and in each ch across. Fasten off.

Position and sew Straps to Sole as desired and as shown in photo.

ANKLE STRAP
With tan, ch 10, sl st in 10th ch from hook to form first loop, continue ch until piece measures 1½ times the length of Sole, ch 10 more, sl st in 10th ch from hook to form 2nd loop, sl st in each ch across to first loop. Fasten off.

DAISY
CENTER
With yellow, ch 2, 7 sc in 2nd ch from hook, **join** (see Pattern Notes) in beg sc. Fasten off.

PETALS
Working in back lps, join white in any sc on Center, [(ch 3, tr, ch 3, sl st) in same st, sl st in next st] around, join in beg sl st. Fasten off.

FINISHING
Using sewing needle and sewing thread, sew Center of Daisy over Toe Straps at point where they cross.

Thread Ankle Strap through Ankle Loop and button loop end of Ankle Strap over Daisy. ■

Ballet Flats

FINISHED SIZES

Instructions given fit size newborn–3 months *(small)*; changes for sizes 3–6 months *(medium)*, 6–12 months *(large)* and 12–18 months *(X-large)* are in [ ].

FINISHED MEASUREMENTS

Sole: 3 inches *(small)* [3½ inches *(medium)*, 4 inches *(large)*, 4½ inches *(X-large)*]

MATERIALS

- Super fine (fingering) weight yarn: 1¾ oz/309 yds/50g each mauve and pink for all sizes
- Size D/3/3.25mm crochet hook or size needed to obtain gauge
- ⅜-inch-wide ribbon: 36 inches

GAUGE

5 sc = 1 inch; 5 sc rows = 1 inch

PATTERN NOTES

You may want to apply a rubber backing on bottom of Sole for toddler sizes if used on floors other than carpet.

Chain-2 at beginning row or round counts as first double crochet unless otherwise stated.

Join with slip stitch as indicated unless otherwise stated.

INSTRUCTIONS
SHOE
MAKE 2.
TOE

Rnd 1: Beg at center of Toe, with mauve, ch 4, sl st in first ch to form ring, ch 3 *(counts as first dc and ch-1)*, [dc in ring, ch 1] 8 times, **join** *(see Pattern Notes)* in 2nd ch of beg ch-3. *(9 sc, 9 ch-1 sps)*

Rnd 2: Ch 1, sc in first st, sc in each ch sp and in each st around, join in beg sc. Fasten off. *(18 sc)*

Rnd 3: Working in **back lps** (*see Stitch Guide*), join pink with sc in any st, ch 3, [sc in next st, ch 3] around, join in beg sc. Fasten off.

Row 4: Now working in rows, join mauve in any ch sp, **ch 2** (*see Pattern Notes*), dc in same ch sp, 2 dc in each of next 12 ch sps, leaving rem ch sps unworked, turn. (*26 dc*)

Row 5: Ch 1, sc in each st across, turn.

Row 6: Ch 2, dc in next st (*ch 2 and dc count as first dc dec*), [**dc dec** (*see Stitch Guide*) in next 2 sts] across, turn. (*13 dc*)

Row 7: Ch 1, sc in each st across, turn.

Row 8: Ch 2, dc in each of next 3 sts, dc dec in next 5 sts, dc in each of last 4 sts, turn. (*9 dc*)

Row 9: Ch 1, sc in each st across. Leaving long end, fasten off.

Fold last row in half, using long end, sew sts tog.

SOLE
Rnd 1: Join mauve with sc in end of row 4 at right-hand side of Toe, ch 1, [sc in next ch-3 sp on rnd 3, ch 1] 5 times across front of Toe, ch 1, [2 sc in end of each dc row and at center fold, sc in end of each sc row] around, ending with sc in same sp as first sc, join in beg sc, **turn**. (*6 ch-1 sps, 23 sc*)

Row 2: Ch 1, sc in each sc across to opposite side of Shoe, leaving sts at top of toe unworked, turn. (*18 sc*)

Row 3: Ch 1, sc in each st across, turn.

Next rows: Rep row 3 until Sole measures size needed or desired length. At end of last row, fasten off.

HEEL
Row 1: With WS of Sole facing, sk first 6 sts, join mauve with sc in next sc, sc in each of next 4 sc, **sc dec** (*see Stitch Guide*) in next 2 sts, sl st in next st, turn.

Row 2: Sk sl st, sc in each of first 5 sts, sc dec in last sc on row 1 and next sc on last row of Sole, sl st in next sc, turn.

Rows 3–6: Rep row 2 until all sts on last row of Sole are worked.

SIDE EDGING
Ch 1, sc in first st, sc in each st and in end of each row around top edge of Shoe, sk all ch-1 sps at front of toe, join in beg sc, turn.

HEEL LOOP
Row 1: Ch 1, sc in each of first 6 sts across Heel, turn. (*6 sc*)

Rows 2–6: Ch 1, sc in each st across, turn.

Row 7: Fold row 6 down on outside, working through both thicknesses, sl st in each st across. Fasten off.

FINAL EDGING
Join pink in any sc of Side Edging near Heel, sl st in each st around, working sl st between sts of Edging rnd below Heel Loop, join in beg sl st. Fasten off.

FINISHING
Cut ribbon in half. Thread through Heel Loop.

Tie in bow around ankle. ∎

Three-Stripe Tennis Shoes

SKILL LEVEL

INTERMEDIATE

FINISHED SIZES

Instructions given fit size newborn–6 months *(small)*; changes for sizes 6–12 months *(medium)* and 12–18 months *(large)* are in [ ].

FINISHED MEASUREMENTS

Sole: 3½ inches *(small)* [4 inches *(medium)*, 4½ inches *(large)*]

MATERIALS

- Light (DK) weight yarn: 1¾ oz/132 yds/50g each white and blue for all sizes
- Size D/3/3.25mm crochet hook or size needed to obtain gauge
- Tapestry needle

GAUGE

5 sc = 1 inch; 5 sc rows = 1 inch

PATTERN NOTES

You may want to apply a rubber backing on bottom of Sole for toddler sizes if used on floors other than carpet.

Work in back loops on Sole unless otherwise stated.

Join with slip stitch as indicated unless otherwise stated.

INSTRUCTIONS
SHOE
MAKE 2.
SOLE

Row 1: With white, ch 7 [7, 8], sc in 2nd ch from hook and in each ch across, turn. *(6 [6, 7] sc)*

Rows 2–5 [2–6, 2–7]: Working in **back lps** *(see Stitch Guide and Pattern Notes)*, ch 1, sc in each st across, turn.

Row 6 [7, 8] (inc): Ch 1, 2 sc in first st, sc in each st across with 2 sc in last st, turn. *(8 [8, 9] sc)*

Rows 7–10 [8–12, 9–14]: Ch 1, sc in each st across, turn.

Row 11 [13, 15] (inc): Ch 1, 2 sc in first st, sc in each st across with 2 sc in last st, turn. *(10 [10, 11] sc)*

Rows 12–15 [14–18, 16–21]: Ch 1, sc in each st across, turn.

Rows 16 & 17 [19 & 20, 22 & 23]: Ch 1, sc in first st, sk next st, sc in each st across to last 2 sts, sk next st, sc in last st, turn. At end of last row, **do not fasten off**. *(6 [6, 7] sc at end of last row)*

Last rnd: Working in sts and in ends of rows around, ch 1, evenly sp sc around, **join** *(see Pattern Notes)* in beg sc. Fasten off.

SIDES

Row 1: With blue, ch 6, sc in 2nd ch from hook and in each ch across, turn. *(5 sc)*

Rows 2–7 [2–10, 2–13]: Ch 1, sc in each st across, turn.

Row 8 [11, 14]: Ch 1, sc in each st across, **changing color** *(see Stitch Guide)* to white in last st, turn.

Row 9 [12, 15]: Ch 1, sc in each st across, turn.

Row 10 [13, 16]: Ch 1, sc in each st across, changing to blue in last st, turn.

Row 11 [14, 17]: Ch 1, sc in each st across, changing to white in last st, turn.

Rows 12–14 [15–17, 18–20]: Rep rows 9–11 [12–14, 15–17].

Rows 15 & 16 [18 & 19, 21 & 22]: Rep rows 9 and 10 [12 and 13, 15 and 16].

Rows 17–31 [20–34, 23–37]: Ch 1, sc in each st across, turn.

Row 32 [35, 38]: Rep row 8 [11, 14].

Rows 33–38 [36–41, 39–44]: *Rep rows 9–11 [12–14, 15–17], rep from * once.

Rows 39 & 40 [42 & 43, 45 & 46]: Rep rows 9 and 10 [12 and 13, 15 and 16].

Rows 41–47 [44–53, 47–59]: Ch 1, sc in each st across, turn.

Row 48 [54, 60]: Ch 1, sc in each st across. Leaving long end, fasten off.

Using long end, sew first and last rows tog. Seam is heel of Side.

BOTTOM EDGING

Working in ends of rows around Sides, join blue with sc at bottom of heel, evenly sp sc around, join in beg sc. Fasten off.

TOP EDGING

Working in ends of rows on rem edge of Sides, join blue with sc at upper edge of heel, evenly sp sc around, join in beg sc. Fasten off.

HEEL LOOP

Row 1: Working over 4 center sts at back of heel, join blue with sc in first st, sc in each of next 3 sts, turn.

Rows 2–5: Ch 1, sc in each st across, turn. At end of last row, fasten off.

UPPER TOP TRIM

Mark center 16 sc at toe, working through both thicknesses, to secure Heel Loop to top of Side, fold Heel Loop to inside, join white at back of heel, sl st in each of next 3 sts at base of Upper

Edging, sl st in each sc around side edge to marked center 16 sts at toe, working through both thicknesses, sl st in first and 8th st at same time, sl st in 2nd and 7th st at same time, 3rd and 6th sts at same time, and 4th and 5th sts at same time top of toes reached, working in rem center 8 sc back toward inside of Shoe, ch 1 this is where the Tongue will be joined, sl st in 4th and 5th sts at same time, 3rd and 6th sts at same time, 2nd and 7th at same time, and first and 8th at same time, continue to sl st in each st along rem side of upper back to heel, join in beg sl st. Fasten off.

JOINING TRIM
Holding Sole and Side pieces tog, with Sides facing, working through both thicknesses, using white, sl st Sides to Sole. Fasten off.

TONGUE
Row 1: Join blue with sc in ch-1 sp at front of toe, 2 sc in same ch sp, turn. *(3 sc)*

Row 2: Ch 1, 2 sc in each st across, turn. *(6 sc)*

Rows 3 & 4: Ch 1, 2 sc in first st, sc in each st across with 2 sc in last st, turn. *(10 sc at end of last row)*

Rows 5–8: Ch 1, sc in each st across, turn.

Row 9: Ch 1, sc in first st, sk next st, sc in each st across to last 2 sts, sk next st, sc in last st, turn. *(8 sc)*

Row 10: Ch 1, sc in first st, sk next st, sc in each st across to last 2 sts, sk next st, sc in last st. Fasten off. *(6 sc)*

TONGUE EDGING
Working across 3 sides of Tongue in ends of rows and in sts, join white with sl st in end of row 1, evenly sp sl st across to opposite end of row 1. Fasten off.

SHOELACE
MAKE 2.
With white, leaving long end for knot, ch 75 or to desired length. Leaving long enough end to tie knot, fasten off.

Tie ends in knot.

Weave Lace through sl sts of Upper Top Trim on top of Shoe above Tongue. Tie ends in bow. ■

Basic
Mary Janes

SKILL LEVEL

INTERMEDIATE

FINISHED SIZES

Instructions given fit size newborn–3 months (*small*); changes for sizes 3–6 months (*medium*), 6–12 months (*large*), 12–18 months (*X-large*), 18–24 months (*2X-large*), 24–30 months (*3X-large*) and 30–36 months (*4X-large*) are in [ ].

FINISHED MEASUREMENTS

Sole: 3 inches (*small*) [3½ inches (*medium*), 4 inches (*large*), 4½ inches (*X-large*), 5 inches (*2X-large*), 5½ inches (*3X-large*), 6 inches (*4X-large*)]

MATERIALS

- Medium (worsted) weight yarn: 1¾ oz/88 yds/50g each gray for Sole on all sizes, and pink for Sides on sizes 2X-large, 3X-large and 4X-large
- Fine (sport) weight yarn: 1¾ oz/176 yds/50g pink for Sides on sizes small, medium, large and X-large
- Size F/5/3.75mm crochet hook or size needed to obtain gauge
- Sewing needle
- Matching sewing thread
- Small buttons: 2
- Stitch markers

GAUGE

Medium weight yarn: 5 sc = 1 inch; 5 sc rows = 1 inch

PATTERN NOTES

You may want to apply a rubber backing on bottom of Sole for toddler sizes if used on floors other than carpet.

Chain-2 at beginning row or round counts as first double crochet unless otherwise stated.

Join with slip stitch as indicated unless otherwise stated.

INSTRUCTIONS
SHOE
MAKE 2.
SOLE

Row 1: With gray, ch 7 [7, 8, 9, 9, 9, 9], sc in 2nd ch from hook and in each ch across, turn. (6 [6, 7, 8, 8, 8, 8] sc)

Rows 2–4 [2–5, 2–6, 2–7, 2–8, 2–9, 2–10]: Ch 1, sc in each st across, turn.

Row 5 [6, 7, 8, 9, 10, 11] (inc): Ch 1, 2 sc in first st, sc in each st across with 2 sc in last st, turn. (8 [8, 9, 10, 10, 10, 10] sc)

Rows 6–8 [7–10, 8–12, 9–14, 10–16, 11–18, 12–20]: Ch 1, sc in each st across, turn.

Row 9 [11, 13, 15, 17, 19, 21] (inc): Ch 1, 2 sc in first st, sc in each st across with 2 sc in last st, turn. (10 [10, 11, 12, 12, 12, 12] sc)

Rows 10–12 [12–15, 14–18, 16–21, 18–24, 20–27, 22–30]: Ch 1, sc in each st across, turn.

Rows 13 & 14 [16 & 17, 19 & 20, 22 & 23, 25 & 26, 28 & 29, 31 & 32] (dec): Ch 1, sc in first st, sk next st, sc in each st across to last 2 sts, sk next st, sc in last st, turn. At end of last row, **do not fasten off**. (6 [6, 7, 8, 8, 8, 8] sc at end of last row)

EDGING

Working in sts, ends of rows and in starting ch on opposite side of row 1, ch 1, evenly sp sc around, **join** (see Pattern Notes) in beg sc. Fasten off.

SIDES

Rnd 1: Using fine weight pink yarn for sizes small, medium, large and X-large, and medium weight pink yarn for sizes 2X-large, 3X-large and 4X-large, mark center st at heel of Sole, join in same st, **bpdc** (see Stitch Guide) around same st, bpdc around each st around, join in beg bpdc.

Rnd 2: Ch 2 (see Pattern Notes), dc in each of next 7 sts, sc in each st across to last 8 sts, dc in each of last 8 sts, join in 2nd ch of beg ch-2.

Rnd 3: Mark center 22 sc at toe, ch 1, sc in each st around to first marker, [sk next 2 sc, dc in each of next 3 sts] 4 times, sk next 2 sts, move markers with each rnd, sc in each st around, join in beg sc.

Rnd 4: Ch 1, dc in next st (first ch-1 and dc count as first dec), [dc dec (see Stitch Guide) in next 2 sts] 3 times, sc in each st across to first marker, 2 dc in center dc of each dc group across toe, sc in each st around to last 8 sts, [dc dec in next 2 sts] 4 times, join in beg dc.

Rnd 5: Ch 1, sc in each st across to first marker, [sk next st, dc in next st] 4 times, sc in each st around, join in beg sc. Fasten off.

STRAP
MAKE 2.

Join fine yarn for smaller sizes and medium for larger sizes to sc at side of Sides above toe on left side for left Shoe and on right side for right Shoe, ch 12, sl st in 5th ch from hook to form buttonhole, sl st in each ch across, sl st in side of Sides to join. Fasten off.

FINISHING

Using sewing needle and sewing thread, sew button in place on opposite side of Shoe from Strap.

Pull Strap across and button in place. ∎

Stitch Guide

For more complete information, visit **FreePatterns.com**

ABBREVIATIONS

beg	begin/begins/beginning
bpdc	back post double crochet
bpsc	back post single crochet
bptr	back post treble crochet
CC	contrasting color
ch(s)	chain(s)
ch	refers to chain or space previously made (e.g., ch-1 space)
ch sp(s)	chain space
cl(s)	cluster(s)
cm	centimeter(s)
dc	double crochet (singular/plural)
dc dec	double crochet 2 or more stitches together, as indicated
dec	decrease/decreases/decreasing
dtr	double treble crochet
ext	extended
fpdc	front post double crochet
fpsc	front post single crochet
fptr	front post treble crochet
g	gram(s)
hdc	half double crochet
hdc dec	half double crochet 2 or more stitches together, as indicated
inc	increase/increases/increasing
lp(s)	loop(s)
MC	main color
mm	millimeter(s)
oz	ounce(s)
pc	popcorn(s)
rem	remain/remains/remaining
rep(s)	repeat(s)
rnd(s)	round(s)
RS	right side
sc	single crochet (singular/plural)
sc dec	single crochet 2 or more stitches together, as indicated
sk	skip/skipped/skipping
sl st(s)	slip stitch(es)
sp(s)	space/spaces/spaced
st(s)	stitch(es)
tog	together
tr	treble crochet
trtr	triple treble
WS	wrong side
yd(s)	yard(s)
yo	yarn over

Chain—ch: Yo, pull through lp on hook.

Slip stitch—sl st: Insert hook in st, pull through both lps on hook.

Single crochet—sc: Insert hook in st, yo, pull through st, yo, pull through both lps on hook.

Front post stitch—fp: Back post stitch—bp: When working post st, insert hook from right to left around post st on previous row.

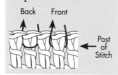

Front loop—front lp Back loop—back lp

Half double crochet—hdc: Yo, insert hook in st, yo, pull through st, yo, pull through all 3 lps on hook.

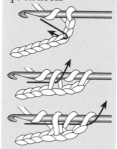

Double crochet—dc: Yo, insert hook in st, yo, pull through st, [yo, pull through 2 lps] twice.

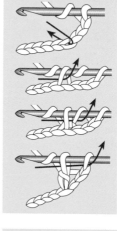

Change colors: Drop first color; with 2nd color, pull through last 2 lps of st.

Treble crochet—tr: Yo twice, insert hook in st, yo, pull through st, [yo, pull through 2 lps] 3 times.

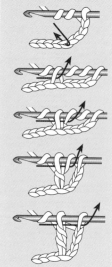

Double treble crochet—dtr: Yo 3 times, insert hook in st, yo, pull through st, [yo, pull through 2 lps] 4 times.

Single crochet decrease (sc dec): (Insert hook, yo, draw lp through) in each of the sts indicated, yo, draw through all lps on hook.

Example of 2-sc dec

Half double crochet decrease (hdc dec): (Yo, insert hook, yo, draw lp through) in each of the sts indicated, yo, draw through all lps on hook.

Example of 2-hdc dec

Double crochet decrease (dc dec): (Yo, insert hook, yo, draw loop through, draw through 2 lps on hook) in each of the sts indicated, yo, draw through all lps on hook.

Example of 2-dc dec

Example of 2-tr dec

Treble crochet decrease (tr dec): Holding back last lp of each st, tr in each of the sts indicated, yo, pull through all lps on hook.

US		UK
sl st (slip stitch)	=	sc (single crochet)
sc (single crochet)	=	dc (double crochet)
hdc (half double crochet)	=	htr (half treble crochet)
dc (double crochet)	=	tr (treble crochet)
tr (treble crochet)	=	dtr (double treble crochet)
dtr (double treble crochet)	=	ttr (triple treble crochet)
skip	=	miss

Metric Conversion Charts

METRIC CONVERSIONS

yards	x	.9144	=	metres (m)
yards	x	91.44	=	centimetres (cm)
inches	x	2.54	=	centimetres (cm)
inches	x	25.40	=	millimetres (mm)
inches	x	.0254	=	metres (m)

centimetres	x	.3937	=	inches
metres	x	1.0936	=	yards

INCHES INTO MILLIMETRES & CENTIMETRES (Rounded off slightly)

inches	mm	cm	inches	cm	inches	cm	inches	cm
1/8	3	0.3	5	12.5	21	53.5	38	96.5
1/4	6	0.6	5 1/2	14	22	56	39	99
3/8	10	1	6	15	23	58.5	40	101.5
1/2	13	1.3	7	18	24	61	41	104
5/8	15	1.5	8	20.5	25	63.5	42	106.5
3/4	20	2	9	23	26	66	43	109
7/8	22	2.2	10	25.5	27	68.5	44	112
1	25	2.5	11	28	28	71	45	114.5
1 1/4	32	3.2	12	30.5	29	73.5	46	117
1 1/2	38	3.8	13	33	30	76	47	119.5
1 3/4	45	4.5	14	35.5	31	79	48	122
2	50	5	15	38	32	81.5	49	124.5
2 1/2	65	6.5	16	40.5	33	84	50	127
3	75	7.5	17	43	34	86.5		
3 1/2	90	9	18	46	35	89		
4	100	10	19	48.5	36	91.5		
4 1/2	115	11.5	20	51	37	94		

KNITTING NEEDLES CONVERSION CHART

Canada/U.S.	0	1	2	3	4	5	6	7	8	9	10	10½	11	13	15
Metric (mm)	2	2¼	2¾	3¼	3½	3¾	4	4½	5	5½	6	6½	8	9	10

CROCHET HOOKS CONVERSION CHART

Canada/U.S.	1/B	2/C	3/D	4/E	5/F	6/G	8/H	9/I	10/J	10½/K	N
Metric (mm)	2.25	2.75	3.25	3.5	3.75	4.25	5	5.5	6	6.5	9.0

RETAIL STORES: If you would like to carry this pattern book or any other DRG publications, visit DRGwholesale.com.

Every effort has been made to ensure that the instructions in this publication are complete and accurate. We cannot, however, take responsibility for human error, typographical mistakes or variations in individual work. Please visit AnniesCustomerCare.com to check for pattern updates.

ISBN: 978-1-59635-310-7

56789